Spilling Ink

Darrielle Cresswell

Little Skye Publishing

Spilling Ink
Little Skye Publishing

Copyright © Darrielle Cresswell 2015

To my family....all of you.
To my friends...all of you.

Acknowledgements:

I would like to thank all the significant people in my life, the experiences I have had, and the plethora of words available, without you, none of these poems would have been written.I would also like to thank my pen and ink.

Spilling Ink

Darrielle Cresswell

Contents

Part 3

PART 1

Spilling Ink

Ink spills,
Splats
And splashes.
Curling words
With dots
And dashes,
It leaks to the page
Through thoughts
In my head
Exposing them all
So they can be read.
Ink is spilling
The page is filling,
Ink has spilled,
Poem fulfilled.

Words

So come hither words of comfort
Wrap me in your onomatopoeia.
Lull me with your lullaby
And rock me with your rhythm
So that I may gently rest
Under your poetical blanket
And sleep deeply;
As peacefully
As a soulful sonnet.

Five minute ditty

If pen is to paper
As paper is to ink
And thoughts are to writing
As script is to think,
Then if ink is a-lacking
Or even the thought,
I will have empty sheets
'Stead of words, there'll be nought.

Purging the Pain

The more I write
The less the pain.
The less the pain
The less I write
Till the pain is eased
And no words come.

Inspiration

Poem do not fear me,
For though I know you well,
You are foreign.
Take whatever shape you please
And illuminate with your colours.
Be perfection in your essence and your end.
In this way your beauty will long be cherished
And desires will be fulfilled.

My books and I

As I open the door
I smile to myself
At all the books upon the shelf.
There's Hughes and Bowen
And Wilfred Owen;
Midst the best of the fiction
Books about diction,
Old books from my youth
some would say were uncouth.
There are books about travel
And ancient lands,
Each one is loved
And spends time in my hands.
You can keep all your trinkets,
The gems, the flash car,
For with my books
I travel,
The farthest, by far.

Writing Flow

Like a limpet
Clinging to the rock,
The pen clings
To the page.
As the waves ebb
To and fro
The limpet remains
Steadfast
Rock steady
And still.
As the pen ebbs and flows
On the page
Movement takes place,
So the limpet
And his rock
Are transported
To another place.

The writer's right

The right to write
And the right to read
Is the sort of right
I essentially need,
For without my pen
And without my book
I'm a fisherman
Without a hook.

Inside Out

Deep inside
A poem resides
Then starts to beg
And shout
To leave its place of safety,
To enter the world,
Get out.
It is a very tricky time
Its shape and form unknown;
For it formulated
Deep within
And exits fully grown.
Until it greets the light of day
There is no way of knowing
If I will like its final shape
Hidden since day of sowing.
But out it must
Else I may burst
For another's already growing.

Creation

Pen poises
Finger ready
To allow the ink to flow.
Words on paper
As thoughts emerge
How it happens
I'll never know.
But it would be tragic
If this magic
Were ever
To get up
And go.

PART 2

Too Late

I knew you were dying,
  I said "I'll be there,"
But the ward was chaotic:
  I started to despair.
The drugs round took ages
  The phone, it did not stop,
Relatives relentless
  I felt that I may flop;
An admission, very septic
  Then one had a fall;
I meant to get back
  But events made me stall.
I outed a buzzer
  Then went to your bed
But one glance
  And I knew,
You were already dead.
  The tears started falling,
As I wondered why
  Life's chaos and utter madness
  Stopped me saying, *goodbye*.

A stormy moment

The wind's in the willows
My heart is in two.
I sit being billowed
Thinking of you.
The wind's in the willows
It's starting to rain
I sit getting drenched
Both with droplets and pain.

A Life well spent.

Is it too late?
To enter in
The inner sanctum
Deep within,
For each second that tolls
Is one more that's extolled,
One less to explore
Life's riches galore.
And before life is spent
All feelings must vent
To extinguish the pain
Of life lived in vain.

Abandoned Draft

I hung upon your every word
Every sentence.
I danced to the tune of your circadian rhythm
Your 'half an hour' and 'two secs'
Finding myself
In you.
Exposed, I allowed myself to become
Part of the Plot;
Catapulted to lead character.
You wrote me some nice lines,
And I trusted the flow of your pen.
I bathed in the glory of the role.
And found myself
For the first time.
I wanted to absorb your thoughts,
Play out my part,
And become indelible
Like the ink on your page.
But as you wrote me in
You began to write me out.
Past plots and characters emerged
Stronger, more vibrant;
Taking away the colour and shape of me,
Chasing me into shadow,
Into the abandoned draft
In the corner, screwed up.

Black Holes

An atom collided
A spark ignited it.
A flame was born.
White heat;
Its heat pulsated;
Sucking into its core
All matter beside it.
Its energy immense,
Its destiny eternal,
Its beauty heavenly.
Purity in its rawest form.
A burning soul;
Eager in anticipation
For the knowledge yet to come.
But the thoughts brought chaos,
The feelings negativity,
Experience disillusion
And the fire began to dim.

Confusion

Where is the reason?
Where is the rhyme?
I need to find it
I need the time
To solve the puzzle,
To ease this razor-sharp pain
In my brain.

Solitary confinement

Of all the things
I've ever known
I do know this
To be alone
Is much the worst-
A living curse;
A space of gloom
A room of doom
Where feeling's numb
And speech struck dumb-
There is no need
No-one to heed
Just the shadow's face
And empty space,
With smiles locked in
Lips sealed and thin,
The laughter dead
From fear and dread.

The Journey

The bus was a womb.
   And I was her foetus.
As we travelled along,
   The darkness descended.
And the cold became colder.
   But I was safe,
Enveloped in warmth,
   Secure in an amnion sac.
I knew no fear,
   And felt no pain.
But the journey ended.
   And my birth took place.

The Struggle

Pressure weighs heavily within,
Head heavy.
My body aches with the stress and the strain
Of knowing that struggling
And striving to succeed
Is often completely in vain.

The Tightrope

Life is one long tightrope.
At times it is stretched
So far that it shakes
And quivers with the strain.
At times it snaps,
And stays broken forever.

Unstuck

I've come unstuck
Because of you
I've come unstuck
I need strong glue.
The type that lasts
Is what I need;
I've come unstuck
You didn't heed
The cracks appearing
In my whole
The widening fissures
In my soul.
You went away
You ceased to care,
I've come unstuck
My heart's laid bare.

Mum

My eyes sting
with the tears
At the thought
Of you.
The air is thin,
And it's hard to breathe.
The ache within is ceaseless.
And everything's in shadow.
You left,
Through no fault of your own.
You raged against it.
Your pain in leaving
Continues still,
In the one left behind.
Relentless,
Remorseless,
Cracking the soul
Wide open,
So no safety remains.

Mum 2

I take down the peg bag
Frayed at the edges
And faded with time.
Perhaps, in taking the pegs out
One by one,
The answers will reveal themselves to me;
For you, my mother,
handled these pegs
On many a sunny day;
And now that the dark clouds
Conspire against me
Hemming me in
To a claustrophobic corner,
I seek the sunshine you felt.
I seek the warmth
That you oozed,
And the soft protective hands
That made everything
Hurt less.
Perhaps, in touching these pegs,
My heirloom from you,
I may touch your wisdom
And find the answers
To dispel this blackness,
Dry up these tears,
And iron out my hurts
In the wind.

Disaster

Tidal wave
Screaming
Undoing
Nature
Annihalating
My
Ink.

PART 3

Listen

Listen
Is *silent*
In letters
Stop
Shouting.
Hear
Me.

A good read

What wisdom within
The covers I found
What beautiful prose
I read
It will always remain
And always sustain
Long after
I'm dead.

If only

If only your touch
Didn't mean as much
If only you felt as I,
Then the rain
Would stop
And the clouds abate
And the sun would
Be in the sky.

Favourites

Oh Cat in the Hat
I loved your rhyme
Back in the days
Of being nine.
My granddaughter Lily
Loves you too
And she is only touching two;
And Peter rabbit
With his jacket
Still is a hero
Of mine,
He got into trouble
And broke all the rules
Yet still came out
Of things fine.
And I cannot forget
The faraway tree
That took me to special places
So full of wonder for little minds
And saucepans
Instead of faces.
Then Alice alighting
A little bit frightening
Encountering so many creatures
What links them all
Is their enduring trait
Of totally magical
Features.

Reflection

I look in the mirror
And what do I see
An old lady smiling,
Looking at me;
The eyes are quit baggy
The chin is all saggy
With skin that crinkles
With the folds of the wrinkles.
I move nearer to look
Like a well thumbed book
This face full of tears
The sum of its years.

Funny bone

He really tickled her funny bone,
A chortle, a smirk and guffaw.
He did it again, knowing full well
She'd laugh like never before;
A giggle, a shout, hilarity broke out
As she crumpled in half on the floor,
"oh please" she gasped, "please stop this Now,
For I really can't take anymore".
But he couldn't resist, so didn't desist
And did it once again,
So she laughed until her tears ran free
And her funny bone was in pain.

Having words

A word is an important thing
Can set the world to rights,
Can likewise cause indelible harm
Used wrong, in emotional fights;
Is essential in the author's world
Else books would cease to be;
Can be very small and plain
Or exceptionally flowery.
A word is an important thing,
Is used to solve a clue
I am very pleased to have some,
As I'm having words with you.

Sorting out

My hell was his heaven
My heaven, his hell;
Such contrary feelings
And differing thoughts
Were never to bode
That well;
So I promised myself
To sort out the shelf
And keep heaven
And hell apart,
Now the shelf is at peace
The books are at ease
And likewise is my heart.

As One

You speak,
I hear.
You touch,
I feel.
You think,
I know.
You feel,
I sense it;
Love,
Soul deep,
Embedded,
Eternal.

Wonder

If quantums leap
And quarks are able,
And strings unwind
Their lengths of cable;
And protons promise
To unleash their tension,
Then I'm not surprised
By a fourth dimension.

Shadows

For one brief instant
My world was bathed in golden light
You took the common place
And turned it on its head.
So unique
So special.
The shadows receded
In the brilliance of your glow.
New life began to grow.

Shades of love

So shallow,
So fickle,
Fragile, yet iron strong.
What are you that baits, frustrates
Fulfills and thrills ?
You bind yet break
Many a tender heart.
You tease:
Sometimes please.
We are subject to your will,
We, the innocent.
Love you are master of all.

Need Fulfilled

The rain falls gratefully from the heavens.
Steaming with relief,
Its warmth soothes the parched dust;
And gradually devours
The pain of desire.
Likewise, my pain is also eased.
There is comfort in the steady
Rhythm of fulfilment,
And my minds yearning for refreshment
Is transported to the ground's
Vast empire of saturation,
Where it is duly submerged
And gratified.

Escape

Today I stole myself away,
   And took some time for me.
The squirrels rustled round about
   The birds screeched in the tree.
The drone of mowers butted in,
   The dog began to bark
The screech commenced of the car alarm
   As someone tried to park.
Today I stole myself away
   And took some time for me.
Twas not a space of tranquil calm
   But a parkland jamboree.

The poet's beat

The beat of the poet
Is something I know, it
Follows me round
Indenting its sound.
A constant low hum,
Then the bang of its drum.
It knows full well
I'm under its spell,
No place I can hide in
For within it's residing.
It will only recede
When I tend to its need
Of exposing its rhyme
in the fullness of time.

Son speak

Upon the stairs I listen in
 Less conversation
More a din
"whats happnin bro ?"
Shouted down the phone
Did I teach him this language
No, its his own
"that's wicked..man"
Has something gone wrong?
No, he seems to be smiling...
And is grunting along..
"Cheers man..That's really safe"
Was something in danger?
Was it nearly too late ?
He seems really pleased
I don't understand
The language he's speaking
From some other land,
And now it is "sick"
And what does he mean?
I want explanation
But I can't intervene
He thinks he's alone
Just him on the phone
So I stay very still
And wonder, who's ill?

Dry Ink

Ink dries;
A poem,
A stain;
A permanent
Print on the page
From my brain.
Ink is drying
A poem is dying,
Though the letters
Remain,
With the splats
Of my crying.
Ink has dried.
Last poem
Supplied.

Made in the USA
Las Vegas, NV
13 August 2024